The Holy Mole

Cookbook

Discover 40 of the Best-Ever
Guacamole Recipes; Appetizers, Dips,
Spreads, and Salads

BY

Daniel Humphreys

License Notes

Table of Contents

Introduction

Guac- a Holy Mole! It's time to celebrate guacamole.

Here, are some fun foodie facts about this delicious dip, amazing appetizer, sensational spread or salad.

- The Aztecs are responsible for inventing guacamole in the 1500s. In fact, they believed it to be an aphrodisiac

- Guacamole Day takes place every year on September 16th
- Sri Lankans enjoy guacamole as a sweet dessert by mashing and mixing avocado with milk, syrup or sugar
- Guacamole is a favorite dip to enjoy on Super Bowl Sunday, and Cinco de Mayo and its popularity has resulted in an increase of US sales of avocados
- Fresh guacamole is the shortest film ever nominated for an Oscar (2012). The animated short film by Adam Pesapane runs for just 1 minute and 40 seconds.
- Fifty years ago, in 1965 saw Hollywood legend and king of horror Vincent Price and wife Anne publish their very own cookbook. A Treasury of Great Recipes includes Vincent's very own favorite guacamole recipe which includes Worcestershire Sauce
- On 6 April 2018, as part of Tancitaro, Mexico's 7th Annual Avocado Festival onlookers saw the largest guacamole serving ever. Over 350 people helped to prepare the gargantuan 8351.11-pound serving

The Holy Mole Cookbook brings together the best ever collection of 40 guacamole recipes to get the party started.

Asparagus and Ancho Chile Guacamole

A super-healthy vegetable, asparagus is good for the brain, and can even help you to lose weight. Combined with hot chilies it makes the greatest-tasting guacamole.

Servings: 4-6

Total Time: 6mins

Ingredients:

- 1 pound asparagus (chopped, steamed)
- 1 ripe avocado (peeled, pitted)
- 1 tbsp jalapeno (minced)
- ⅛ cup cilantro leaves (coarsely chopped)
- 1 tsp ancho chile powder
- 1 tsp celery salt
- 1 tsp cumin
- ½ tsp freshly ground black pepper
- Freshly squeezed juice of 1 lime
- 3 tbsp red onion (peeled, minced)
- ½ cup cherry tomatoes (quartered)

Directions:

1. Add the asparagus, avocado, jalapeno, cilantro leaves, ancho chile powder, celery salt, cumin, black pepper, and lime juice to a food blender and on the pulse setting, process until combined.

2. Transfer to a serving bowl and fold in the minced onions along with the tomatoes.

Avocado and Jicama Dip

Jicama is a Mexican vegetable with an apple-like flavor has a wonderful crunch that gives this dip an addictive texture.

Servings: 6

Total Time: 10mins

Ingredients:

- 3 ripe avocados (peeled, stoned, diced)
- 2 cups jicama (diced)
- Juice of 2 medium limes
- 4 scallions (sliced)
- Salt and black pepper

Directions:

1. Combine the avocado, jicama, lime juice, and scallions in a bowl.

2. Season to taste with salt and black pepper. Serve straight away.

Bell Pepper and Red Onion Guacamole

Both bell pepper and red onion have a natural sweetness that balances this cayenne-spiced guacamole.

Servings: 3

Total Time: 10mins

Ingredients:

- 1½ tbsp red onion (peeled, diced)
- 2 ripe avocados (halved, stoned, mashed)
- 5 baby carrots (peeled, shredded)
- 3 tbsp red bell pepper (seeded, diced)
- ¼ tsp cayenne pepper
- Juice of ½ a medium lemon
- Sea salt and black pepper

Directions:

1. Combine the red onion, avocado, carrot, bell pepper, cayenne pepper, and lemon juice in a large bowl.

2. Taste and season with sea salt and black pepper.

3. Serve straight away.

Blueberry and Tomato Guacamole

Give guacamole a fruity, berrylicious kick and create a sweet and spicy side or dip.

Servings: 4-6

Total Time: 18mins

Ingredients:

- ½ cup fire roasted corn
- 1 tsp avocado oil
- 3 large avocado (peeled, pitted, diced)
- ¼ cup frozen blueberries (thawed)
- 1 garlic clove (peeled, minced)
- ¼ red onion (peeled, diced)
- 1 jalapeno (diced)
- 6 cherry tomatoes (cut into quarters)
- 1 tsp red pepper flakes
- Freshly squeezed juice of 1 lime
- 2 tbsp cilantro (chopped)
- 2 tbsp basil (chopped)
- Salt and black pepper
- 2 tbsp blueberries (to garnish)

Directions:

1. Over moderate heat, in a small frying pan, sauté the corn in avocado oil for 3-5 minutes, until cooked through. Set to one side to cool.

2. In the meantime, add the avocado along with the blueberries to a glass bowl and using a fork, mash until incorporated.

3. Add the sautéed corn along with the garlic, red onion, jalapeno, tomatoes, red pepper flakes, lime juice, cilantro, and basil, mixing to combine entirely.

4. Taste and season with salt and pepper.

5. Garnish with 2 tablespoons of blueberries.

Cheesy Guacamole

Give guacamole a cheesy boost with grated Cheddar cheese. Enjoy this delicious dip with chips.

Servings: 4

Total Time: 15mins

Ingredients:

- 2 ripe avocados (peeled, pitted, diced)
- 1 medium tomato (diced)
- 1 jalapeno pepper (seeded, finely diced)
- Freshly squeezed juice of 1 lime
- ½ cup black beans (drained, rinsed)
- 4 green onions (finely sliced)
- ½ cup sharp, mature Cheddar cheese (grated)
- Salt and black pepper

Directions:

1. Add one of the avocados to a mixing bowl and with a fork, lightly mash.

2. Add the tomatoes followed by the jalapeno, fresh lime juice and gently mix to combine.

3. Add the black beans, onions, grated cheese and the remaining avocado. Stir thoroughly and season.

4. Transfer to the fridge to chill before serving.

Crab Guacamole

Add fresh crab to creamy guacamole and transform a dip into an appetizer.

Servings: 2

Total Time: 15mins

Ingredients:

- 1 large Roma tomato (diced, seeded)
- ½ red onion (peeled, diced)
- 1 clove garlic (peeled, finely minced)
- 1 tbsp cilantro (chopped)
- ½ jalapeno (diced small)
- 2 avocados (peeled, pitted, halved)
- 1 large lime
- 1 tsp cumin
- Sea salt
- Freshly ground black pepper
- 8 ounces fresh crab meat

Directions:

1. Add the tomatoes, onion, garlic, cilantro, and jalapeno to a mixing bowl, mixing to combine. Set to one side.

2. With a fork mash the avocados and combine with the fresh lime juice, cumin, salt, and pepper.

3. A little at a time fold the tomato-jalapeno mixture into the mashed avocado along with the crab.

4. Taste and season.

Creamy Corn Guacamole

Take guacamole to the next level with grilled corn. Serve with tortillas and cold beer.

Servings: 4-6

Total Time: 10mins

Ingredients:

- 4 avocados (peeled, pitted, pulp removed)
- 4 ounces cream cheese (softened)
- 1½ cups grilled corn kernels
- ⅓ cup red onion (peeled, finely chopped)
- ⅓ cup tomato (finely chopped)
- ½ tsp garlic (peeled, minced)
- 1 jalapeno (finely chopped)
- Freshly squeezed juice of ½ lime
- ¼ tsp salt

Directions:

1. In a food blender, process the avocado and cream cheese until creamy smooth.

2. Fold in the corn kernels, red onion, tomato, garlic, jalapeno, and lime juice.

3. Taste and season with salt.

Creamy Lime Guacamole

This guacamole is perfect for sandwiches, as an appetizer or dip or alongside your favorite Mexican dishes.

Servings: 6

Total Time: 7mins

Ingredients:

- 1 ripe avocado (peeled, pitted, mashed)
- ¼ cup fat-free sour cream
- 2 tbsp freshly squeezed lime juice
- 1 tsp Dijon mustard
- ½ tsp hot pepper sauce
- 1 tsp salt
- ¼ tsp cumin
- 2 tbsp fresh cilantro (chopped)

Directions:

1. Add the avocado, sour cream, lime juice, mustard, pepper sauce, salt, cumin and cilantro to a bowl and mash to combine.

2. Cover the bowl and chill until you are ready to serve.

Dill Pickle Guacamole

If you like pickles, you will love this tasty guacamole.

Servings: 6-8

Total Time: 8mins

Ingredients:

- 3 ripe avocados (peeled, pitted, mashed)
- 2 tbsp dill pickle juice
- ½ cup jarred dill pickles (chopped)
- ¼ red onion (peeled, finely chopped)
- 1 clove garlic (peeled, minced)
- 1 tbsp dill (chopped)
- ½ tsp red pepper flakes
- Kosher salt
- Freshly ground black pepper
- Chopped pickles (to serve)

Directions:

1. Add the avocado, pickle juice, chopped pickles, onion, garlic, dill and red pepper flakes to a mixing bowl. Mix to combine. Season to taste.

2. Garnish with additional pickles and serve.

Fajita Guacamole

This dip is perfect for enjoying with friends and family on game night.

Servings: 6-8

Total Time: 10mins

Ingredients:

- ½ tsp olive oil
- ½ red pepper (julienned)
- ½ green pepper (julienned)
- ½ small red onion (julienned)
- ¼ tsp salt
- ⅛ tsp freshly ground black pepper
- ½ tsp cumin
- ½ tsp paprika
- ¼ tsp garlic powder
- ¼ tsp onion powder
- 3 ripe avocados (peeled, pitted)
- Freshly squeezed juice of 1 lime
- 1 clove garlic (peeled, minced)
- ⅓ cup queso fresco cheese (crumbled)
- Salt

Directions:

1. Over moderate heat, heat a pan.

2. Add the olive oil, peppers, along with the red onion, salt, pepper, cumin, paprika, garlic powder and onion powder and cook for 10 minutes, while occasionally stirring. Set aside to cool before chopping into bite-sized pieces.

3. Score the avocado halves with a knife and scoop out the avocado flesh and add to a bowl. Using a fork, mash the avocados.

4. Add the fresh lime juice, onion-pepper mixture, garlic, crumbled cheese and season with salt to taste, mixing until incorporated.

5. Serve.

Feta and Watermelon Guacamole

Sweet watermelon and salty feta bring a Mediterranean twist to this refreshing guacamole.

Servings: 4

Total Time: 10mins

Ingredients:

- ⅓ cup fresh cilantro (chopped)
- 3 large ripe avocados (peeled, stoned, mashed)
- 1 jalapeno pepper (deseeded, minced)
- ¼ cup red onion (peeled, diced)
- ⅓ cup feta cheese (crumbled)
- 2 tbsp freshly squeezed lime juice
- 1 cup seedless watermelon (diced)
- Salt and black pepper

Directions:

1. Combine the cilantro, mashed avocado, jalapeno, red onion, feta, lime juice, and watermelon.

2. Season to taste with salt and pepper and serve straight away.

Fiery Strawberry Guacamole

This fruity guacamole is loaded with hot and fiery jalapeno peppers.

Servings: 8-10

Total Time: 10mins

Ingredients:

- 1 cup fresh strawberries (finely chopped)
- 6 ripe avocados (peeled, stoned, finely chopped)
- 1 cup yellow cherry tomatoes (halved)
- Zest and juice of 2 limes
- ½ cup red onion (peeled, diced)
- 2 jalapenos (seeded, diced)
- 1 cup fresh cilantro (chopped)
- Salt and black pepper

Directions:

1. Combine the strawberries, avocado, tomatoes, lime zest and juice, red onion, jalapeno, and cilantro in a bowl.

2. Season to taste with salt and pepper and serve straight away.

Fig and Bacon Guacamole

Crispy, crumbled bacon adds texture and taste to this creamy creation. Enjoy with tortilla chips for a sweet and salty mouth-watering dip.

Servings: 6

Total Time: 10mins

Ingredients:

- Candied Pecans:
- ¼ cup light brown sugar
- ⅛ tsp salt
- 1 tbsp cold water
- ½ cup pecan halves
- ¼ cup fresh cilantro leaves (finely chopped)

Guacamole:

- 4 ripe avocados (peeled, pitted)
- 2 tbsp freshly squeezed lime juice
- 2 garlic cloves (peeled, minced)
- 5 slices bacon (crispy, crumbled)
- ⅓ cup red onion (peeled, finely chopped)
- ⅓ cup dried mission figs (chopped)
- 1 jalapeno stem (seeded, finely chopped)
- ⅓ cup candied pecans (chopped)
- ⅓ cup blue cheese (crumbled)
- ½ tsp sea salt
- ¼ tsp freshly ground black pepper

To serve:

- Candied pecans (to garnish)
- Blue cheese (crumbled)
- Garnish: a sprinkle of extra candied pecans and blue cheese crumbles

Directions:

1. First, prepare the candied pecans. In a skillet over moderate heat, combine the sugar with the salt and cold water and cook until the sugar entirely dissolves, for between 1-2 minutes.

2. Add the pecans and cook while stirring to evenly coat for a few minutes.

3. Remove from the heat and spread out on a parchment paper lined baking sheet, to dry. Allow to cool, before coarsely chopping. This should yield approximately ⅓ cup.

4. To make the guacamole, spoon the avocado flesh into a bowl, add the fresh lime juice and mash to your desired consistency.

5. Add the garlic followed by the bacon, onion, figs, jalapeno, candied pecans, blue cheese crumbles, sea salt, black pepper, and cilantro. Gently mixing to combine.

6. Serve garnished with candied pecans, and blue cheese crumbles.

Orange Guacamole

Fresh and fruity orange pieces bring fruity flavor to creamy, spicy guacamole to make a party-worthy dip or appetizer.

Servings: 4

Total Time: 1hour 15mins

Ingredients:

- 4 ripe avocados (peeled, pitted, halved)
- 1 large navel orange (peeled, sectioned, cut into 1" pieces)
- 2 tbsp red onion (peeled, finely chopped)
- 3 tbsp fresh orange juice
- 1 jalapeño pepper (seeded, finely chopped)
- 1 garlic clove (peeled, pressed)
- ¾ tsp salt
- Pomegranate arils (to garnish)

Directions:

1. Add the avocado pulp to a mixing bowl and using a fork, mash with a fork, until chunky.

2. Stir in the orange followed by the onion, orange juice, jalapeno pepper, garlic, and salt.

3. Cover the bowl and transfer to the fridge for between 2-4 hours.

4. Serve and garnish with pomegranate arils.

Grilled Guacamole with Parmesan

This modern take on guacamole combines grilled and crispy avocado with garlic, basil, and cheese giving an Italian twist to this otherwise classic recipe.

Servings: 2-4

Total Time: 15mins

Ingredients:

- 3 ripe avocados (peeled, pitted, halved)
- 3 tbsp oil
- Freshly squeezed zest and juice of 1 lemon
- Truffle salt and black pepper
- 1 large garlic clove (peeled, minced)
- ¼ cup loosely packed basil leaves (coarsely chopped)
- ½ cup Parmesan (freshly grated)

Directions:

1. Preheat your panini press to its highest heat setting.

2. Drizzle the avocado halves with olive oil and sprinkle with lemon juice. Season.

3. Arrange the avocado halves, cut side facing down on the panini press and cook until golden and crispy, for approximately 4 minutes.

4. Scoop the flesh out of the avocados, add to a bowl, and with a fork, gently mash.

5. Add the olive oil, lemon zest, seasoning, garlic, basil, and cheese.

6. Serve.

Grilled Peach, Jalapeno, and Bacon Guacamole

Grilled peaches are perfect for adding sweetness to your favorite guacamole while bacon adds a little smokiness.

Servings: 4

Total Time: 20mins

Ingredients:

- 1 ripe peach (cut in half, pitted)
- 2 large, ripe avocados (peeled, pitted)
- 2 slices smoked bacon (cooked, chopped)
- ½ cup white onion (chopped)
- 2 jalapenos (seeded, minced)
- ½ cup cilantro (chopped)
- Freshly squeezed juice of 1 lime
- 1 tsp sea salt

Directions:

1. Preheat the grill to 450 degrees F.

2. Arrange the peach halves, face side facing down on the grill and grill for 2-3 minutes, until charred and softened. Allow to cool before chopping into bite-size pieces and adding to a bowl.

3. Add the avocado to the bowl, and with a fork gently mash.

4. Fold in the cooked bacon, onion, jalapeno, cilantro, lime juice, sea salt, and serve.

Guacamole Potato Salad

No contest, this is the best potato salad, ever featuring creamy avocado instead of mayonnaise making it a healthy choice.

Servings: 6-8

Total Time: 10mins

Ingredients:

- 2 pounds small red potatoes (scrubbed)
- 2 ripe avocados (peeled, pitted, mashed)
- 2 garlic cloves (peeled, minced)
- 2 green onions, whites only (finely chopped)
- 1 large Serrano pepper (seeded, minced)
- ½ tsp salt

Directions:

1. Add the potatoes to a microwave-safe bowl and add sufficient water, to cover.

2. On high, microwave on high for 10 minutes, until fork tender.

3. Drain and transfer to the fridge, until cold.

4. Slice the cooked and cooled potatoes into bite-size pieces and add to a bowl.

5. Stir in the avocado, garlic, green onions, Serrano pepper, and salt.

6. Serve.

Guacamole with Banana and Almonds

This guacamole is a taste sensation. Creamy avocado and banana are perfect pairings with crunchy sliced almonds.

Servings: 2

Total Time: 5mins

Ingredients:

- 2 ripe avocados (peeled, pitted)
- ½ banana (peeled, lightly mashed)
- 2 tbsp tomato (finely diced)
- 2 tbsp red onion (peeled, minced)
- 2 tbsp red pepper (finely diced)
- 2 tbsp sliced almonds
- Freshly squeezed juice and zest of 1 lime
- 1 tbsp cilantro (chopped)
- Salt and pepper

Directions:

1. Add the avocado flesh to a bowl and with a fork, mash until just smooth.

2. Fold in the banana followed by the tomato, onion, pepper, and almonds, stirring to combine.

3. Add the lime zest and juice.

4. Taste and season.

Guacamole with Crispy Pulled Pork

Crispy pulled pork adds texture to this creamy dip which is an ideal buffet party food.

Servings: 4-6

Total Time: 40mins

Ingredients:

- 1 cup pulled pork
- 4 ripe avocados (peeled, pitted)
- 1 jalapeño pepper (seeded, diced)
- ⅓ cup queso fresco cheese (crumbled)
- ¼ cup fresh cilantro (chopped)
- 3 tbsp sweet onion (diced)
- Freshly squeezed juice of 1 lime
- ¼ tsp salt
- ¼ tsp black pepper
- Queso fresco cheese (crumbled, to serve)

Directions:

1. Preheat the main oven to 425 degrees F.

2. Evenly spread the cooked pulled pork in a casserole dish.

3. Place the dish in the oven and roast for between 20-30 minutes, using a fork to toss the pork every 8-10 minutes.

4. Add the avocados, jalapeno, queso fresco cheese, cilantro, sweet onion, fresh lime juice, salt and black pepper to a bowl, and using a fork, mash until combined.

5. Taste and season.

6. Top with the crispy pork, and garnish with additional cheese.

Thai-Style Guacamole with Fish Sauce

The creamy flavor of avocado is enhanced by zesty lime and cilantro while the fish sauce adds depth.

Servings: 2-4

Total Time: 7mins

Ingredients:

- 2 ripe avocados (peeled, pitted)
- 1 tbsp freshly squeezed lime juice
- 1 tsp Thai fish sauce
- ¼ tsp sea salt
- 2 tbsp fresh cilantro (chopped)

Directions:

1. Add the avocados to a mixing bowl and with a fork, coarsely mash.

2. Add the fresh lime juice followed by the fish sauce and sea salt and mash to combine.

3. Stir in the chopped cilantro and serve.

Guacamole with Roasted Eggplant

Roasted eggplant is flavorsome and moist which makes this guacamole ideal for dipping with chips.

Servings: 3

Total Time: 1hour 30mins

Ingredients:

- 2 eggplants
- Juice of 1 lime
- Salt and garlic powder
- ½ ripe avocado (peeled, stoned, mashed)
- ½ red onion (peeled, diced)
- 2 tbsp fresh cilantro (chopped)
- ½ cup grape tomatoes (quartered)

Directions:

1. Preheat the main oven to 350 degrees F.

2. Arrange the eggplant on a baking tray and place in the oven. Cook for just under an hour until soft. Allow to cool before slicing in half lengthways.

3. Scoop the flesh into a bowl and allow to completely cool.

4. Add the lime juice, salt, garlic powder, avocado, and eggplant to a blender and blitz until smooth.

5. Stir in the red onion, cilantro, and tomatoes. Transfer to a bowl and serve.

Guac-Kale-Mole

An extra healthy and nutritious guacamole made with fresh kale. Did you know that kale has greater nutritional value than spinach?

Servings: 4-6

Total Time: 15mins

Ingredients:

- 5 kale leaves (stemmed, finely chopped)
- 4 medium avocados (peeled, pitted)
- Freshly squeezed juice 1 lime
- Freshly squeezed juice of 1 lemon
- 3 garlic cloves (peeled, minced)
- ½ red onion (peeled, finely chopped)
- 1 jalapeno (cored, finely chopped)
- ¾ cup cilantro (finely chopped)
- 1 Roma tomato (finely chopped)
- ½ tsp sea salt

Directions:

1. Add the kale, avocado, lime juice, lemon juice, garlic, onion, jalapeno, cilantro, tomato and salt to a blender, and process to a chunky consistency.

2. Transfer to the fridge to chill.

3. Serve.

Healthy Guacamole with Broccoli

A great way to get the kids to eat some broccoli!

Servings: 3-4

Total Time: 10mins

Ingredients:

- ¾ cup chopped broccoli florets
- ¼ cup red onion (peeled, minced)
- 1 tomato (diced)
- 1 tbsp fresh lemon juice
- 1 clove garlic (peeled, minced)
- Handful fresh cilantro (roughly chopped)
- 2 ripe avocados (halved, stoned, flesh scooped)

Directions:

1. Toss together the broccoli, onion, tomato, lemon juice, garlic, and cilantro in a bowl.

2. Stir in the avocado until combined.

3. Taste and season as necessary.

4. Enjoy straight away.

Hummus-Guacamole

Our two favorite dips combine in this hummus guacamole hybrid made with chickpeas, avocado, and fresh cilantro.

Servings: 8

Total Time: 1hour 30mins

Ingredients:

- 3 cups fresh cilantro (chopped)
- 1 (15½ ounce) can chickpeas (drained)
- 1 ripe avocado (peeled, stoned, chopped)
- 1 clove garlic (peeled, finely chopped)
- 1 tbsp freshly squeezed lemon juice
- 3 tbsp olive oil
- Water
- Salt and black pepper

Directions:

1. Add the cilantro, chickpeas, avocado, and garlic to a food processor and pulse until finely chopped.

2. With the processor running, slowly pour in the lemon juice and olive oil. Then 1 tbsp at a time, add water until you achieve a smooth consistency.

3. Season with salt and black pepper. Serve straight away.

Italian-Style Guacamole

Mexican guacamole is infused with the Italian flavors of garlic and basil.

Servings: 4-6

Total Time: 10mins

Ingredients:

- 2-3 garlic cloves (peeled, minced)
- 3 ripe avocados (halved, stoned, mashed)
- 1 tomato (diced)
- 1 jalapeno (seeded, diced)
- 1 tbsp fresh lemon juice
- ½ cup red onion (peeled, diced)
- ¼ cup fresh basil (chopped)
- ½ tsp each salt and black pepper

Directions:

1. Combine the garlic, avocado, tomato, jalapeno, lemon juice, red onion, and basil in a large bowl.

2. Taste and season with sea salt and black pepper.

3. Serve straight away.

Jambalaya-Style Guacamole

Guacamole doesn't get much more of a kick to it than this! Andouille sausage, hot sauce, and shrimp bring a Cajun-inspired influence to this creamy dip.

Servings: 6-8

Total Time: 35mins

Ingredients:

- 2 tbsp vegetable oil (divided)
- 3 slices thick bacon
- 4 ounces andouille sausage (coarsely chopped)
- ½ cup yellow onion (peeled, chopped)
- ½ cup celery (chopped)
- ¾ cup red bell pepper (chopped)
- 1 garlic clove (peeled, minced)
- 1 tsp smoked paprika
- ¼ tsp dried thyme
- 1 tsp dried oregano
- ¼ tsp cayenne pepper
- ½ tsp salt
- ½ tsp black pepper
- 1 small Roma tomato (cored, seeded, diced)
- 1 tsp Worcestershire sauce
- Tabasco sauce (to taste)
- ½ pound medium shrimp (peeled, deveined, cut into bite-size pieces)
- 3 ripe avocados (peeled, pitted, diced)
- 2 tsp freshly squeezed lemon juice
- 3 scallions white and light green parts (finely sliced)

Directions:

1. Heat a tbsp of vegetable oil in a baking dish over moderate heat, until hot. Do not allow it to smoke.

2. Add the bacon followed by the sausage and fry while frequently stirring with a spatula or wooden spoon, until crisp and gently browned, for approximately 4-5 minutes.

3. Combine the onion along with the celery, pepper, and garlic. Season with paprika, thyme, oregano, cayenne, salt, and pepper, thoroughly mixing and cooking until softened, for between 3-4 minutes.

4. Add the tomato, Worcestershire sauce and a dash of Tabasco. Stir while cooking for another 60 seconds.

5. Remove from the heat and scrape the mixture into a mixing bowl.

6. Place the same baking dish on high heat and add an additional 1 tbsp of vegetable oil.

7. When sufficiently hot, add the shrimp and season, cooking until gently browned all over but for no more than 60 seconds.

8. Add the shrimp to the mixing bowl containing the other ingredients.

9. In a second smaller bowl, add the diced avocado, and lemon juice and mix gently. Add to the Jambalaya mixture and toss to combine.

10. Scatter the scallions over the top, season with salt and serve.

Mango Guacamole

A sweet and savory guacamole is a tempting topping for burgers, toast or chips.

Servings: 4-6

Total Time:

Ingredients:

- 4 ripe avocados (peeled, pitted)
- 1 medium tomato (chopped)
- ½ cup mango (peeled, pitted)
- ⅓ cup red onion (peeled, chopped)
- 1 jalapeno (seeded, chopped)
- Handful of cilantro
- ½ tsp salt
- ¼ tsp black pepper
- Freshly squeezed juice of 2 medium limes

Directions:

1. Add the avocado flesh along with the tomato, mango, red onion, jalapeno, and cilantro.

2. Season with salt and black pepper and fresh lime juice, mashing until you achieve your preferred consistency.

Margarita-Style Guacamole

Two Mexican favorites come together in this orange and mint-infused guac.

Servings: 4

Total Time: 10mins

Ingredients:

- 3 ripe avocados (peeled, stoned, mashed)
- ½ tsp orange zest (grated)
- 1 tbsp freshly squeezed orange juice
- 2 tbsp freshly squeezed lime juice
- ¼ cup fresh mint
- ¼ cup jalapeno (seeded, diced)
- 2 tsp salt
- ¼ tsp black pepper

Directions:

1. Add the mashed avocado to a bowl along with the orange zest, citrus juices, mint, jalapeno, salt, and black pepper. Stir until well combined.

2. Serve straight away.

Mediterranean Chickpea Guacamole

This Mediterranean guacamole substitutes oregano for cilantro and is wonderful in wraps or sandwiches.

Servings: 2-4

Total Time: 10mins

Ingredients:

- 1½ cups chickpeas (drained, rinsed)
- 4 tbsp freshly squeezed lime juice
- 2 ripe avocados (peeled, pitted)
- Salt (to taste)
- ½ tsp dried oregano
- 1 tomato (diced)
- ¼ cup red onion (peeled, diced)
- 3 tbsp flat leaf parsley (finely chopped)

Directions:

1. Add the chickpeas to a food blender and process to a puree.

2. In a mixing bowl add the fresh lime juice to the avocado flesh, tossing to coat. With a fork, mash to your preferred consistency. Season with salt to taste and add the oregano.

3. Fold in the chickpea puree along with the tomato, onion, and parsley, mixing until fully combined.

4. Transfer to the fridge to chill for 20-30 minutes, to allow the flavors to infuse and serve.

Oven-Roasted Garlic Guacamole

Oven-roasting the garlic really intensifies the flavor of this bold guacamole.

Servings: 4-6

Total Time: 50mins

Ingredients:

- 1 garlic bulb
- Olive oil
- ½ cup fresh cilantro (roughly chopped)
- 4 ripe avocados (peeled, stoned, mashed)
- 1½ tbsp fresh lime juice
- 3 scallions (sliced)
- 1 tsp salt

Directions:

1. Preheat the main oven to 400 degrees F.

2. Cut the head off the garlic to expose the cloves and rub with olive oil. Cover with kitchen foil and cook in the oven for half an hour. Allow to completely cool before scooping out the roasted cloves and set to one side.

3. Combine the cilantro, avocado, lime juice, scallion, salt, and roasted garlic.

4. Taste and add more lime juice as necessary. Enjoy straight away.

Pineapple Salsa Guacamole

Guacamole gets a tropical twist with fresh, and juicy pineapple. A delicious dip to chip with beers, soda or wine.

Servings: 4

Total Time: 12mins

Ingredients:

- 4 ripe avocado (peeled, pitted, mashed)
- Freshly squeezed juice of 1 lime
- 1 cup pineapple (peeled, chopped)
- ¼ cup red onion (peeled, chopped)
- 1 jalapeno (minced)
- 1 garlic clove (peeled, minced)
- Sea salt
- Cilantro (to garnish)

Directions:

1. Mash the avocados with the lime juice, pineapple, red onion, jalapeno, and garlic. Season with salt and serve garnished with cilantro.

Pink Grapefruit Guacamole

Although grapefruit is primarily sharp by using sweet, pink grapefruit the guacamole will have a pleasant citrus tang.

Servings: 6-8

Total Time: 15mins

Ingredients:

- 3 (8 ounce) ripe avocado (peeled, pitted)
- ½ tsp sea salt
- 1 sweet pink grapefruit (cut in half)
- ½ medium jalapeno (seeded, diced)
- 1 yellow onion (peeled, diced)
- ½ tsp cumin
- 1 tbsp cilantro leaves (chopped)

Directions:

1. Add the avocado to a bowl and sprinkle with salt.

2. Squeeze the fresh juice from one-half of the grapefruits over the avocado.

3. Mash the avocado together with the juice until smooth and smooth yet chunky. Set to one side.

4. Remove the flesh from both halves of the pink grapefruit and chop.

5. Using a knife, cut the chopped grapefruit flesh and add it to the avocado-juice mixture.

6. Finally, add the diced jalapeno followed by the onion to the avocado-grapefruit mixture.

7. Top with cumin and chopped cilantro leaves and serve.

Pomegranate Guacamole

Classic guacamole gets a fruity makeover with juicy pomegranate arils and fresh cilantro.

Servings: 6

Total Time: 10mins

Ingredients:

- 2 ripe avocados (halved, stoned, flesh scooped)
- ½ tsp each salt and black pepper
- ¼ cup fresh cilantro (chopped)
- ⅓ cup red onion (peeled, diced)
- ½ cup pomegranate arils
- 2 tbsp fresh lime juice

Directions:

1. Mash the avocado flesh in a bowl and season well.

2. Add the cilantro, onion, pomegranate, and lime juice. Stir until combined.

3. Serve straight away.

Prawn and Dill Guacamole

This guacamole featuring fresh prawns is the perfect appetizer, snack or dip for a party.

Servings: 6-8

Total Time: 9mins

Ingredients:

- 10½ ounces prawns (cooked, peeled, thinly sliced)
- 2 ripe avocado (peeled, pitted, finely chopped)
- 1 tbsp freshly squeezed lime juice
- 2 tbsp dill (finely chopped)
- Salt and pepper

Directions:

1. Add the prawns, avocado, fresh lime juice, and dill to a bowl, gently tossing to combine.

2. Taste and season.

3. Transfer the mixture to a bowl and serve.

Pumpkin Guacamole

Roasted pumpkin brings color and sweetness to this fiery jalapeno guacamole.

Servings: 4

Total Time: 10mins

Ingredients:

- 2 ripe avocados (halved, stoned, mashed)
- 1 tsp olive oil
- ½ cup red onion (peeled, diced)
- 1 tomato (diced)
- ¼ cup fresh cilantro (chopped)
- 1 jalapeno (deseeded, diced)
- ¼ tsp cumin
- 2 tbsp freshly squeezed lime juice
- 2 cups roasted pumpkin (diced)
- Sea salt

Directions:

1. Combine the avocado, oil, onion, tomato, cilantro, jalapeno, cumin, and lime juice in a bowl.

2. Fold in the pumpkin and season to taste with salt.

3. Serve straight away.

Spring Pea and Mint Guacamole

This healthy avocado mash is perfect as a pesto, delicious as a dip and sublime as a spread. It's time to go green!

Servings: 1

Total Time: 7mins

Ingredients:

- ¼ cup fresh spring peas
- ½ tsp coriander seeds
- 2 sprigs of mint leaves
- Sea salt and black pepper
- ⅓ avocado (peeled, pitted)
- 1 lemon wedge

Directions:

1. In boiling water, blanch the pea pods for a few minutes until cooked but al dente. Drain and set to one side.

2. In a pestle and mortar grind the coriander seeds along with the mint and a pinch of sea salt.

3. Add the peas to the pestle and mortar and gently mash.

4. In a second bowl, mash the avocado.

5. Add the pea-mint mixture to the avocado mash and with a fork, carefully combine.

6. Top with lemon juice and season to taste.

Summer Stone Fruit Guacamole

This gorgeous guacamole provides a real taste of summer. Enjoy with tortilla chips, spread on wraps or enjoy with grilled chicken.

Servings: 4-6

Total Time: 8mins

Ingredients:

- 2 ripe avocado (peeled, pitted)
- 3 tbsp freshly squeezed lime juice
- Salt
- 1 cup sweet nectarines (pitted, diced)
- ½ cup ripe plums (pitted, diced)
- ½ cup red onion (peeled, diced)
- ¼ cup fresh basil (chopped)

Directions:

1. Add the avocados to a bowl and with a fork, mash.

2. Add the fresh lime juice and a pinch of salt. Mix to combine.

3. Finally, add the nectarines, plums, onion, and basil, stirring to combine.

Toasted Pepita and Cotija Cheese Guacamole

Toasted pumpkin seeds (pepitas) bring crunch while punchy cotija cheese ramps up the flavor.

Servings: 4-6

Total Time: 10mins

Ingredients:

- 2 tbsp freshly squeezed lime juice
- 3 ripe avocados (peeled, stoned, mashed)
- ¼ cup jalapeno pepper (seeded, diced)
- ¼ cup red onion (peeled, diced)
- ½ cup fresh cilantro (chopped)
- Salt and black pepper
- 4 tbsp cotija cheese (crumbled)
- ¼ cup pepitas (toasted)

Directions:

1. Combine the lime juice, avocado, jalapeno, red onion, and cilantro in a bowl.

2. Season to taste with salt and black pepper.

3. Sprinkle over the cotija cheese and toasted pepitas, serve straight away.

Tuna Guacamole

This guacamole with tuna is tasty and satisfying enough to eat all on its own.

Servings: 2

Total Time: 10mins

Ingredients:

- ½ ripe avocado (peeled, stoned, mashed)
- 1 (5 ounce) can tuna in water (drained)
- Juice of ½ a medium lime
- ½ tsp cumin
- 1 tbsp fresh cilantro (chopped)
- 1 tbsp red onion (peeled, diced)
- ¼ cup diced tomatoes
- ¼ tsp powdered garlic
- Salt and black pepper

Directions:

1. Combine the avocado, tuna, lime juice, cumin, cilantro, onion, tomatoes, and garlic in a bowl.

2. Season to taste with salt and pepper and serve straight away.

Vincent and Anne Price's Guacamole

This guacamole recipe is based on the original 1965 version by British born, king of horror, Vincent Price and his wife Anne. It features Worcestershire sauce.

Servings: 2-4

Total Time: 10mins

Ingredients:

- 2 avocado pears (peeled, pitted, pit reserved)
- 3 tbsp freshly squeezed lemon juice
- 1 small onion (peeled, finely chopped)
- 1 small green chili (finely chopped)
- ⅛ tsp ground coriander
- ½ clove garlic (peeled, minced)
- Salt to taste
- 3 tbsp mayonnaise
- Tomato (peeled, chopped, seeded)
- 1 tsp Worcestershire sauce
- Dash of cayenne or Tabasco

Directions:

1. Using a fork mash the avocado. Add the lemon juice, onion, green chili, coriander, garlic, salt to taste, mayonnaise, tomato, Worcestershire sauce and a dash of cayenne or Tabasco.

2. Leave the pit in the mixture until you are ready to serve, as this helps to prevent the mixture from discoloring.

3. Alternatively, remove the pit and add the ingredients to a food blender and on high blend for 8 minutes.

4. Serve.

Author's Afterthoughts

Thanks ever so much to each of my cherished readers for investing the time to read this book!

I know you could have picked from many other books but you chose this one. So a big thanks for downloading this book and reading all the way to the end.

If you enjoyed this book or received value from it, I'd like to ask you for a favor. Please take a few minutes to post an honest and heartfelt review on Amazon.com. Your support does make a difference and helps to benefit other people.

Thanks!

Daniel Humphreys

About the Author

Daniel Humphreys

Many people will ask me if I am German or Norman, and my answer is that I am 100% unique! Joking aside, I owe my cooking influence mainly to my mother who was British! I can certainly make a mean Sheppard's pie, but when it comes to preparing Bratwurst sausages and drinking beer with friends, I am also all in!

I am taking you on this culinary journey with me and hope you can appreciate my diversified background. In my 15 years career as a chef, I never had a dish returned to me by one of clients, so that should say something about me!

Actually, I will take that back. My worst critic is my four years old son, who refuses to taste anything that is green color. That shall pass, I am sure.

My hope is to help my children discover the joy of cooking and sharing their creations with their loved ones, like I did all my life. When you develop a passion for cooking and my suspicious is that you have one as well, it usually sticks for life. The best advice I can give anyone as a professional chef is invest. Invest your time, your heart in each meal you are creating. Invest also a little money in good cooking hardware and quality ingredients. But most of all enjoy every meal you prepare with YOUR friends and family!

Made in the USA
Coppell, TX
23 March 2020